# PERFECTIONISM

A step-by-step approach to overcoming perfectionism and procrastination head on

Carol Sloan

# CONTENTS

"When no-one around you seems to measure up,

it's time to check your yardstick"

Bill Lemley

# INTRODUCTION

Perfectionism is often viewed as a positive trait that can increase one's chances of achieving success in both their personal and professional life. It is important to note that being a perfectionist is not necessarily a bad thing and doesn't need to be eliminated altogether. However, it does have a downside that can lead to behaviors and thoughts that can be defeating and make it more challenging to achieve one's goals. Additionally, individuals may experience mental health issues like depression, anxiety, and stress due to perfectionism.

This book provides a comprehensive understanding of what perfectionism is, its causes, and symptoms. Readers will learn how to differentiate the various forms of this trait, along with its advantages and disadvantages. While perfectionism can lead to success, if it is indeed working for you, then keep it. On the other hand, if things are not going as planned, taking time to pause and reflect on what could be done differently is essential. This book highlights how perfectionism can be both useful and detrimental to one's life.

Perfectionism is directly linked to anxiety and poor mental health. This book sheds light on the factors related to how being a perfectionist can cause such mental health problems and how to cope with them. Many people suffer from OCD due to perfectionism, and this book provides ways to manage anxiety or help friends who are struggling with perfectionism.

# CHAPTER 1: THE PERFECTIONISM LANDSCAPE

Perfectionism is the belief that you can achieve perfection, or the desire to appear perfect, and is often considered a key trait in achieving success. For some, it is an integral part of their personality that they do not want to eliminate. However, for others, it can hinder success and lead to suffering and failure. Some use perfectionism as a shield against blame, shame, and judgment.

Some people are perfectionists all the time, while others only engage in it depending on the situation. How do you know if you or your loved one is a perfectionist? There are signs that can help identify this trait. For example, if you are a perfectionist, you may not start a task until you feel you can do it perfectly, and you may focus more on the end result rather than the process or learning. You may also experience procrastination because you will not start a task until you can complete it without flaw, which can lead to taking more time to complete tasks than necessary.

Common examples of perfectionism include spending an excessive amount of time writing and re-writing a two-sentence email, feeling like a failure for missing only a couple of points on an exam, difficulty being happy for others' success, unrealistic and unfavorable comparisons to others, and avoiding tasks or skipping classes because you feel like you cannot achieve perfection.

Perfectionism can lead to success for some, but it can also have negative consequences. To manage its impact on your life, the first step is to recognize the signs of perfectionism.

## Different types of perfectionism

Perfectionism comes in both adaptive and maladaptive forms. Those with adaptive forms of perfectionism always strive for success, setting high work standards and working hard to complete their tasks on time. They don't overdo their strengths or limitations. In contrast, those with maladaptive perfectionism become obsessed with achieving a perfect performance and find nothing satisfactory. They apply their high standards to other people's behaviors as well. People with maladaptive perfectionism may avoid taking on tasks for fear of not completing them on time or without making an error.

There are three main types of perfectionism, each with similar behaviors but different outcomes and motives:

**Self-critical perfectionism**: Those with self-critical perfectionism are intimidated by their own goals and feel hopeless about their ability to achieve them. This type of perfectionism leads to negative emotions like anxiety, distress, and self-condemnation.

**Socially prescribed perfectionism:** People with socially prescribed perfectionism demand excellence and are often found in fields like medicine, law, and architecture. They may experience stress, hopelessness, and are prone to self-harm and suicide. This type of perfectionism can also arise from high societal and cultural standards that are difficult to meet, such as academic expectations set by parents.

**Personal standards perfectionism:** Those with personal standards perfectionism set their own standards of perfection and are motivated by meeting them. This type of perfectionism is considered healthy as it doesn't lead to burnout or excessive stress and doesn't involve harmful habits to manage anxiety.

If your goals energize you instead of overwhelming you, you may have this type of perfectionism. Recognizing the signs and types of perfectionism is the first step in managing its impact on your life.


## Causes of Perfectionism


Perfectionism can have many causes, and one of the leading causes is the belief that a person's self-worth is based on their achievements. However, there can be a combination of causes for perfectionism, and sometimes parental pressure since early childhood may also be a cause. Children whose parents have rigid or high expectations or are shaming, critical, or abusive may become perfectionists when they grow up, developing the need for excessive praise for their achievements.

Low self-esteem and cultural expectations can also cause perfectionism. Here are some common causes of perfectionism:

**Negative Reinforcement**: Negative reinforcement from parents or mentors is often used to teach children respect, responsibility, and manners. However, in some cases, this negative reinforcement results from a desire or expectation of parents or mentors for perfection, putting pressure on children. They might feel disappointed, wrong, or bad and develop a desire to be perfect.

**Aspiration for reward**: As children, we are given rewards when we do something well, creating a desire to receive more rewards. This desire for acceptance and rewards can later turn into perfectionism.

**Mimicked behavior**: Another common cause of perfectionism is learned behavior. As children, we learn by copying the adults around us, and we can adopt perfectionist traits from our parents, mentors, etc. Some families even encourage perfectionism by punishing children for not getting straight A's, leading them to grow into adults who are perfectionists.

It's important to recognize the underlying causes of perfectionism so that we can work to manage its impact on our lives.

## Symptoms of Perfectionism

Desiring to achieve something is not unhealthy, but when the desire is to be perfect at all times, it may become irrational and cause serious problems. How can you tell if you are suffering from a perfectionism disorder? The following symptoms can indicate this:

- A feeling that you will fail every time you try.
- Procrastination: you avoid beginning a task because you fear you will not finish it perfectly.
- Difficulty relaxing or sharing your thoughts and feelings.
- Displaying controlling behavior in your personal or professional relationships.
- Becoming apathetic or obsessed with rules, work, lists, and so on.
- Feeling frustrated and giving up quickly on assigned tasks.
- Anxiety about making a mistake.
- Fear of embarrassment or being looked down upon if the task is not done correctly.

## Real Life Stories: One Woman's Journey to Self-Acceptance

As a child, Sarah was always driven to excel in everything she did. Her parents had high expectations, and Sarah always strived to meet them.

They would praise her when she did well, but whenever she made a mistake, they would become upset and disappointed. Over time, Sarah's need to be perfect became overwhelming, and it began to affect her life negatively.

One day, Sarah was asked to give a presentation in front of her class. She had prepared extensively and had rehearsed her speech many times, but as soon as she stepped in front of the class, her mind went blank. She stumbled on her words and forgot her lines. She felt embarrassed and ashamed, and her heart sank as she saw her classmates' disappointed faces.

From that day on, Sarah's fear of making mistakes only grew worse. She started procrastinating on her schoolwork, avoiding any task that she feared she could not complete perfectly. She became more withdrawn and found it difficult to relax and enjoy life.

It wasn't until Sarah started seeking help that she realized she was struggling with perfectionism. She learned that her fear of failure was limiting her growth and keeping her from reaching her full potential. With the right support, Sarah was able to overcome her perfectionism and find a healthier balance in her life.

# Quiz: How much of a Perfectionist are You?

Read each statement and then decide which number on the scale of 1 to 5 most reflects your opinion.

1 = Never  2 = Rarely  3 = Sometimes true

4 = Often true  5 = Always true

- I find myself obsessing over the finer details of a task.
- I find myself checking and rechecking my work before considering it finished.
- I avoid trying things that I might not be good at.
- I find it challenging to make decisions.
- I believe that if I don't do well all the time, people won't respect me.
- I worry more than most people do.
- I have been called critical or picky.
- People think that I'm too fussy.
- I find it difficult to delegate tasks because I believe that it's unlikely anyone else will do it correctly.
- I feel like I have to do everything myself because I don't believe anyone else can do things properly.
- I become upset when others don't meet my standards.
- I can't stand being interrupted.

- I avoid going out in public unless I'm well-dressed.
- I'm afraid that people will look down on me if I look foolish or make a mistake.

Identify the questions where you scored yourself 4 or 5. If the number of questions that scored 4 or 5 is greater than 7, then you are very much a perfectionist. For each of those questions, ask yourself whether this characteristic causes difficulty in your relationships, work, or leisure, or if it interferes with your ability to enjoy life generally. If you answer "yes" to even one or two questions, you will benefit from learning how to change.

# CHAPTER 2: IS ALL PERFECTIONISM BAD?

People often believe that being perfect is the solution to every problem in their life. They strive to achieve perfection in all areas without realizing that there are disadvantages to perfectionism as well. Refer to the list below to evaluate whether being a perfectionist is benefiting your life or causing problems.

## Pros of Perfectionism

**Increased ambition and motivation**: As a perfectionist, you would set high standards and goals for yourself. This would make you highly ambitious and motivated to reach those goals. You would be willing to do anything to achieve perfection in meeting your ultimate goals.

**Higher social status**: Perfectionism can improve your social status because people around you will become aware of your abilities and seek your help when the need arises.

**Improved work performance**: Obviously, as a perfectionist, you would strive to do excellent work, resulting in high-quality work. You would aim to ensure that your work was as good, if not better, than others.

**Chances of being a role model**: As a perfectionist, you would be recognized in your social circle due to your high work standards. People would consider you a role model, admiring and respecting you for your dedication to perfection.

**Increased perseverance:** Perfectionists try to get through challenging situations as their levels of motivation and ambition are high. Therefore, their levels of determination are also high.

**Greater emphasis on details**: Perfectionists pay attention to small and minute details, which is not everyone's forte. In most work cases, this strength would make them an asset to a work team.

## Cons of Perfectionism

**Less cost-effective:** Perfectionists do not benefit the company economically, as they are slow in their work, causing them to produce less work than others. They take a lot of time to make a project perfect, and not just good, which may negatively affect the company's bottom line.

**Unhappiness**: Perfectionists are never happy with anything they do. They worry about missing details, which can cause them to feel quite anxious and unhappy inside.

**Harmful for your career**: As perfectionists, your output levels are low, which puts your job at risk.

While others might complete several tasks simultaneously, you only focus on one to make it flawless, jeopardizing your career and causing you harm.

**Unnecessary pressure:** Perfectionists have this unnecessary pressure on their head all the time to excel. Even tasks like washing their bathrooms can take more than an hour because they want it to be spotless. And if they fail, they begin to feel stressed.

**Chances of social isolation**: As perfectionists spend most of their time doing tasks and chores, they might miss opportunities to go to social gatherings, leading to social isolation.

**Inability to prioritize:** Perfectionists are unable to prioritize. When they have two tasks simultaneously, they find it difficult to allocate their time effectively. Instead, they would waste time on one task while leaving the other one incomplete, leading to a lack of effective time management.

**You may become annoying**: Perfectionism always leads to frustration, anxiety, and irritability. You might seem to be annoyed and irritated as you may feel under pressure all the time, becoming annoying to those around you.

**Chronic stress**: Perfectionists usually suffer from chronic stress. This occurs when they feel they have to achieve their desired goals no matter what. They may encounter stress-related disorders, sleep deprivation, and may even experience severe depression. Most perfectionists suffer from Obsessive-Compulsive Disorders.

**Your mood may be negatively affected**: Perfectionists may always be edgy. Due to the pressure to be perfect in everything they do, their physical and mental health might be affected, which can impact their mood. They may become extremely irritable, sad, and miserable at different points in time.

**Fear of failure:** Perfectionists always have a fear of failure. No matter how hard they work, they would still be scared if their work is not up to the mark. They would have a feeling that something is missing, and now the entire project is worthless.

## Problems that arise due to being a perfectionist

For a perfectionist, there is always something more to achieve than what they have already accomplished. This can be both an advantage and a cause of many problems. Perfectionists have many issues that affect the people around them. Some of the common issues that arise due to perfectionism are:

**Relationship problems**. Perfectionists go through a lot of relationship problems, and the people around them suffer as well. For instance, if they are in a romantic relationship, their partners may feel inadequate due to the high demands and expectations of perfectionists. Perfectionists can quickly feel resentful, disappointed, and angry in relationships, making it difficult to be around them. Although they are very gracious and supportive of their friends, there are times when they can become very rigid, competitive, and passive-aggressive. Only friends who can understand and cooperate with them can develop long-term relationships with them.

**Anxiety issues.** As perfectionists always feel unsatisfied with everything they do, they frequently think they need to do better and develop a tendency to feel anxious. They can continuously feel anxious, which could further develop into depression or other emotional issues. We will briefly discuss the personal issues related to perfectionism in the next chapter.

**Procrastination.** The biggest problem that perfectionists face is procrastination. They could delay doing a task just because they feel they wouldn't be able to do it correctly at that time. This could lead to severe problems like failing an exam or getting fired. They could waste hours of their precious time just because they cannot meet their own standards. This problem affects their careers and lifestyles and may also affect the organization they are a part of.

**Intolerance of mess and disorganization.** Perfectionists cannot tolerate any sort of disorganization or mess. They have a particular ideal in mind regarding everything. If it is not according to what they have in mind, it could lead them to feel toxic and negative. This also generates feelings of shame within them if they are not able to organize their surroundings.

**Sense of self-worth.** A perfectionist can either have a high sense of self-worth or feel they are not good enough. In most cases, they believe they are not up to their standards, which is why they keep trying to do better. However, this could lead to an obsession. Their sense of self-worth comes from the perfect output and a sense of achievement. If perfectionists believe they have achieved the best outcome, they expect to be appreciated and loved for being perfect. If the people around them do not follow suit, it could lead to severe consequences.

## Real Life Stories: The Perfectionist's Dilemma

Lily was a hardworking and ambitious person who always strived for perfection in every aspect of her life. From her work to her relationships, she had high standards that were often difficult to meet.

One day, Lily had planned a surprise picnic for her boyfriend, Tom. She had spent hours perfecting the menu, choosing the right location, and making sure everything was in place. However, when Tom arrived, he noticed that the picnic basket was not perfectly aligned with the blanket. He pointed it out to Lily, who immediately began to feel anxious and frustrated.

Lily became so consumed by her need for perfection that she couldn't enjoy the picnic with Tom. Instead, she spent the entire time worrying about the small imperfections and feeling upset that she couldn't meet her own high standards. By the end of the day, Tom had had enough and told Lily that he couldn't continue their relationship if she continued to place such unrealistic expectations on herself and others.

Lily realized that her perfectionism was not only causing problems in her personal life but also affecting her own happiness. She decided to seek help and learned how to manage her perfectionism better. She learned that it was okay to make mistakes and that imperfection was a natural part of life.

After that day, Lily knew that overcoming her perfectionism would be a lifelong journey. She sought out therapy and read books on the topic, actively working to strike a balance between her drive for excellence and her need for a healthy and fulfilling life. Although she still had moments of anxiety and frustration, she no longer let her high standards control her life and relationships.

Eventually, Tom and Lily rekindled their relationship, but it wasn't without its challenges. Lily still struggled with her perfectionism from time to time, and Tom had to be patient and supportive as she worked through those moments. However, with time, they learned to communicate better and build a stronger, more resilient relationship.

## Activity: Reduce Unhelpful Thinking

One helpful and balanced way to improve your thinking is by using a thought diary. These diaries are specifically designed to help you become more aware of negative thoughts and how they affect your emotions and behavior.

To begin, create your own thought diary by using sheets of paper. Divide each sheet into six sections and label them as follows:

- Situation/Trigger
- Emotions (Rate 0 to 100%)
- Physical sensations
- What did I think?
- Response
- What could I have done & thought

**Notes**:

Ask yourself what emotions you were feeling during the event. There may be several different emotions, but choose the most dominant one and rate its intensity from 0 to 100. (The higher the number, the more intense the feeling.)

- What thoughts were going through your head at that time? Choose the dominant thought that is most closely connected to your emotions.
- What actions / behaviors did you engage in?
- What physical sensations did you experience?

- Don't try to challenge all your unhelpful
  thoughts and beliefs at once. Take them on
  one by one. Underline your dominant thought
  and rate how much you believe this thought,
  between 0 and 100.
- Identify any unhelpful thinking styles that might
  be in operation.
- Ask yourself questions such as: "How might
  someone else, who is not a perfectionist, view
  the situation? How else could I view the
  situation?

# CHAPTER 3: PERFECTION AND ITS TOLL ON MENTAL HEALTH

Saying that you're a perfectionist may create a positive image, but what's beneath the surface is often overlooked. If left unchecked, perfectionism can have a devastating impact on your mental and physical health. Perfectionists can experience a range of mental health issues, including anxiety, depression, and even suicidal thoughts. Obsessive-Compulsive Disorder is also a common challenge faced by perfectionists.

Negative thought patterns and emotional distress are a common experience for perfectionists. The fear of not meeting their high standards can lead to feelings of shame, low self-esteem, and anxiety. If left unaddressed, these feelings can even escalate to suicidal tendencies.

Moreover, perfectionism can create a distorted belief that one is not worthy of love and acceptance from others, despite being a role model for others. Even when others praise their work, perfectionists can struggle to accept that they are good enough.

If you're struggling with perfectionism, there are steps you can take to mitigate its negative impact on your well-being. One effective strategy is to practice self-compassion, which involves treating yourself with kindness and understanding when things don't go according to plan. Learning to set realistic goals and expectations for yourself can also help you avoid burnout and cultivate a healthier relationship with your work. Lastly, seeking support from loved ones, friends, or a mental health professional can provide you with the tools and guidance necessary to navigate the challenges of perfectionism. Remember, you don't have to struggle alone, and there is always help available.

## Is perfectionism a sign of low self-esteem?

Perfectionism can take a toll on one's mental health, and a major reason for this is related to self-esteem. When your self-esteem is low, your defense mechanisms can kick in, and perfectionism may become a way to boost your confidence. You may feel inadequate and try to compensate by striving to be the best at everything, whether it's getting the highest grades or being the top employee in your workplace. Unfortunately, this kind of pressure can lead to perfectionism.

As a perfectionist, you may set extremely high standards for yourself, which can result in unrealistic goals. For instance, you may aim for a 99% score on your math exam and still feel like a failure. Perfectionists tend to see things in black and white and cannot settle for anything less than perfect. As a result, they may easily become disappointed and upset with themselves over minor mistakes or perceived shortcomings.

It's important to realize that perfectionism is a sign of low self-esteem and, if not managed properly, can lead to serious mental health issues. Small steps like recognizing your perfectionistic tendencies, setting realistic goals, and celebrating your accomplishments, no matter how small, can help break the cycle of perfectionism and improve your overall well-being. Remember, it's okay to make mistakes and learn from them. Embracing imperfection can lead to greater creativity and personal growth.

## The link between perfectionism and anxiety

The connection between perfectionism and anxiety is undeniable. The fear of making mistakes and facing negative consequences leads to anxiety in individuals. Perfectionists have an innate desire to avoid mistakes and do everything to the best of their ability. However, this desire for perfection can be detrimental to their mental health. Perfectionists are often obsessed with achieving their goals and can experience anxiety as a result.

Anxiety disorders and perfectionism go hand in hand, with two types of anxiety disorders often being related to perfectionism: Generalized Anxiety Disorder and Social Anxiety Disorder. Generalized Anxiety Disorder involves a fear of failure or not being worthy of something, which can lead to overwhelming worry over different aspects of life. On the other hand, Social Anxiety Disorder involves an obsession with how others perceive an individual. Perfectionists may experience high levels of social anxiety, fearing embarrassment or rejection due to not being good enough.

Perfectionists tend to see things as absolutes, with no grey area. This black and white thinking can contribute to anxiety, as any mistake or deviation from their standards can feel like a failure. Perfectionists may also fear being scolded or reprimanded for their errors, leading to an anxiety-inducing cycle of perfectionism.

Overall, perfectionism can contribute to anxiety disorders and other mental health issues. It is crucial to recognize the signs of perfectionism and take steps to address it before it becomes a more significant problem. Seeking support and practicing self-compassion can help individuals manage their perfectionistic tendencies and promote better mental health.

## OCD and Perfectionism

Dealing with perfectionism can be challenging, but what if you're also dealing with Obsessive-Compulsive Disorder (OCD)? For those unfamiliar, OCD is an unhealthy form of perfectionism that often develops from perfectionism. Here are some common signs of OCD:

**Rigid demands for things to be done a certain way**

Perfectionism is helpful to a certain extent, but when it becomes an obsession, it can be detrimental to your well-being. You may have OCD if you believe things must be done the way you see fit, and anything less is unacceptable.

**Excessive checking behavior**

If you feel the need to check and recheck everything, such as if the stove is turned off or if the door is locked, you may be experiencing OCD symptoms. The fear of making a mistake or feeling uncertain can lead to abnormal checking behavior that can be distressing.

**Need for control**

If you feel the need to control everything, including your thoughts and surroundings, you may have OCD. A person with OCD may find certain ideas or thoughts distressing and feel compelled to control them.

If you or someone you know has OCD perfectionism, they may engage in repeated behaviors, despite knowing they are irrational or unnecessary. This behavior can be detrimental to one's self-confidence and lead to increased anxiety and stress.

# How to cope with OCD?

Recognizing and coping with obsessive-compulsive tendencies can be a daunting task. However, there are some things you can do to manage your condition. If seeking medical advice is not your first option, there are a few things you can try on your own. But, if things seem out of control, it is best to seek help from a medical professional.

## Here are a few things you can try to cope with OCD:

### Mindfulness Meditation

Practicing mindfulness meditation can be very helpful. This technique promotes living in the present moment, which can help you become more aware of your emotions and thoughts. It will help you calm down and reduce anxiety, which will help you become less obsessed with perfection. All you have to do is find a quiet place to sit, relax, and focus on your breathing for 15 minutes daily.

### Cognitive Behavioral Therapy

Cognitive behavioral techniques can also help you manage your OCD. This type of therapy includes cognitive restructuring and behavioral experiments, which can help you learn that it is okay to make mistakes and accept flaws. Cognitive therapy also helps you examine your beliefs critically. It includes exposure and response prevention, which can help you tolerate a loss of control.

However, the most effective way to cope with OCD is to talk to a therapist and seek their advice. They can provide you with personalized guidance and strategies to help you overcome your OCD tendencies. Remember, seeking help is a sign of strength, not weakness.

# CHAPTER 4: THE PROCRASTINATION-PERFECTIONISM PARALYSIS

Perfectionism can have a significant impact on our ability to take action, leading to a vicious cycle of procrastination and stress. It can be especially challenging for perfectionists to start tasks because they are paralyzed by the fear of not doing it perfectly.

Even small tasks such as sorting out old clothes or organizing files can seem overwhelming and time-consuming, causing perfectionists to put them off indefinitely. And when it comes to more significant projects that require greater risk, commitment, and time, procrastination becomes an even more significant problem.

Unfortunately, procrastination can have negative consequences in many areas of life. Perfectionists may delay updating their resumes, taking on new challenges, or pursuing personal goals, and this can leave them feeling stuck and unfulfilled.

It's easy to come up with excuses for not taking action, such as being too busy or having too much work to do. But these excuses only serve to hold us back, and they become convenient crutches that prevent us from making meaningful changes in our lives.

By recognizing the connection between perfectionism and procrastination, we can start to take steps to break the cycle. One effective strategy is to focus on progress rather than perfection and take small steps towards our goals every day. This can help build momentum and create a sense of accomplishment that motivates us to keep moving forward.

# 8 Steps to Beat Procrastination

## Step 1: Focus on one task at a time

As a perfectionist, it's common to feel like you won't do a task correctly, which can lead to procrastination. To increase your focus, take one thing at a time. If you're facing a large project, divide it into smaller, more manageable tasks. Then, focus on completing one task at a time, taking short breaks between each to boost your concentration.

For instance, if you're a student with eight exams to study for, concentrate on one exam at a time. If the course outline is too daunting, break it down into smaller portions. The smaller goals you set, the easier it will be to achieve them. Celebrate reaching milestones with a short break. This way, you'll feel satisfied by completing something and motivated to do more.

## Step 2: Create a to-do list

Make a habit of listing the things you need to complete each day, prioritizing the most important to least important tasks. This approach will help you understand what you have to do and from where you should start. A to-do list is especially helpful for perfectionists who may find numerous tasks challenging to cope with.

For example, list the activities you need to do today and prioritize them. Check off each task as soon as you complete it to give yourself a sense of accomplishment.

## Step 3: Create a detailed timetable

Create a timetable for a day or week with specific details, including the activities you need to do and the amount of time you have to allocate for each. Break down larger tasks and projects into smaller tasks and allocate them to the timetable with an allocated time. This way, you can finish projects on time, and a more significant job won't seem so intimidating.

## Step 4: Stay organized

Proper scheduling and organization throughout the day will help you reduce procrastination. Make sure you have all the tools and materials you need to complete each task on hand, so you don't have to search for items in the middle of your work. When we don't have everything sorted out, procrastination becomes easier.

For example, if you have a deadline to meet, break the project into smaller tasks, so it doesn't feel overwhelming. Keep the most difficult tasks for when you're most efficient, whether that's in the morning or at night. This way, you'll finish them more quickly.

## Step 5: Start taking action

Perfectionism often leads to procrastination due to the fear of not doing something correctly. No matter how daunting a task may seem, start it and finish it. Once you begin working on it, it will become easier to complete.

For example, if you're assigned a project, start working on it right away, so you get closer to finishing it. When you start, adopt the good-enough approach and work within a specified time frame.

## Step 6: Use the Eisenhower Matrix

The Eisenhower Matrix is a simple technique that helps to end procrastination. Create four different boxes and categorize them with urgent and important tasks, important but not urgent, urgent but not important, and neither urgent nor important. The first box should list urgent and important tasks that need to be done immediately. The second box should contain important but not critical tasks to schedule later. The third box should include tasks that are urgent but not important, which can be delegated to someone else, and the fourth box should list tasks that are neither urgent nor important, which can be eliminated to reduce the burden.

The Eisenhower Matrix will help you prioritize tasks quickly, as it helps people tackle challenging or difficult tasks that they may otherwise procrastinate over.

## Step 7: Boost self-motivation

Perfectionists often lack the motivation to complete tasks. Boosting your motivation will subsequently decrease procrastination. There are several ways to boost your self-motivation:

**Set realistic goals:** As a perfectionist, you might be tempted to set unrealistic goals for yourself, which can lead to frustration and procrastination. Instead, set achievable goals and break them down into smaller, manageable tasks.

**Celebrate small wins:** Acknowledge and celebrate your progress, no matter how small. This will keep you motivated and make you feel accomplished, which will help you stay on track.

**Visualize success:** Take a few moments to visualize yourself successfully completing your task. Imagine how you will feel once it's done and how it will benefit you in the long run.

**Find your why:** Understanding why you want to complete a task can be a powerful motivator. Make a

list of the reasons why this task is important to you
and refer to it when you feel demotivated.

**Reward yourself:** Treat yourself after completing a
task or achieving a milestone. It can be something as
simple as taking a break or something more
substantial like buying yourself a gift.

## Step 8: Practice self-compassion

Perfectionists tend to be extremely hard on
themselves. Practicing self-compassion can help you
reduce your inner critic and improve your mental
health. Here are a few ways to practice self-
compassion:

Treat yourself like you would treat a friend: When
you're being hard on yourself, ask yourself, "What
would I say to a friend in this situation?" and give
yourself the same kind of encouragement.

Practice mindfulness: Mindfulness can help you
become more aware of your thoughts and feelings
without judgment. When you notice negative self-talk,
take a deep breath and focus on the present moment.

Forgive yourself: Nobody is perfect, and everyone
makes mistakes. When you make a mistake,
acknowledge it, learn from it, and move on. Don't beat
yourself up over it.

Practice gratitude: Focusing on what you're grateful for can help you shift your perspective and cultivate a more positive mindset.

Take care of yourself: Make sure you're taking care of your physical and emotional needs. This includes getting enough sleep, exercise, and healthy food, as well as engaging in activities that bring you joy.

By following these steps, you can learn to manage your perfectionism and overcome procrastination. Remember that progress takes time and effort, so be patient and kind to yourself as you work towards your goals.

## Real Life Stories: Breaking Free from Perfectionism

Meet Sophie, a dedicated professional who always strived for perfection in everything she did. She believed that this was the secret to her success. But little did she know that this obsession was slowly taking a toll on her mental and physical health.

One day, while giving an important presentation, Sophie stumbled and felt her carefully crafted slides failing her. Her perfectionism prevented her from seeing the situation objectively and caused her to feel devastated. That's when she realized that her approach was no longer serving her well.

She revisited an article she had read on perfectionism and decided to try the eight steps for overcoming it. Sophie adopted healthier alternatives, such as embracing excellence and adopting the good enough approach. She started to notice a positive change in her attitude towards herself and her work, becoming more productive, self-aware, and compassionate towards herself and others.

Let Sophie's story inspire you to embrace a healthier mindset and to realize that perfectionism is not the key to success. Rather, it can be a roadblock to personal growth and happiness. Remember, it's a journey, but it's worth it.

# CHAPTER 5: A COUPLE OF HEALTHY ALTERNATIVES TO PERFECTION

Living with perfectionism can be exhausting and can drain you both physically and mentally. It can make you feel like you're never good enough and doubt your self-worth. It's hard to be gracious to yourself or accept compliments from others when you constantly feel like you're not measuring up.

Perfectionists often experience frustration or agitation when they make mistakes or fail to live up to their standards. Additionally, they may struggle to delegate tasks to others because they find it difficult to trust anyone else to do things to their level of perfection.

However, there are alternatives that can help perfectionists find relief from these frustrations:

## Excellence

Instead of striving for perfection, aim for excellence. Excellence allows for imperfections and leaves room for growth and improvement. By embracing the idea of excellence, you'll be less hard on yourself and be open to learning and discovering more about yourself, your environment, and the people around you. When you make a mistake, you can learn from it and use it as an opportunity for growth, instead of obsessing over it.

Adopting a mindset of excellence also enables you to show yourself and others more grace and understanding. This approach allows you to treat people with compassion and kindness when they make mistakes or do things differently from how you would do them.

## The Good Enough Approach

The second alternative is the "good enough" approach. This approach encourages you to accept that sometimes, doing your best is all you can do. When you feel like you can't do something to your high standards, aim for doing something that is good enough.

In conclusion, adopting a mindset of excellence and using the good enough approach are healthy alternatives for perfectionists. By making these changes, you'll be able to manage your perfectionism and find greater satisfaction and contentment in your life.

Here are some strategies that perfectionists can use when moving towards excellence and the good enough approach:

**Set realistic goals:** Instead of striving for perfection, set achievable goals that are aligned with your values and priorities.

**Break tasks into smaller steps:** Break down larger tasks into smaller steps and focus on completing them one at a time. This can help you feel less overwhelmed and make progress towards your goals.

**Celebrate progress:** Instead of focusing only on the end result, celebrate the progress you make along the way. Recognize your efforts and acknowledge your achievements.

**Practice self-compassion:** Be kind and supportive to yourself, even when things don't go as planned. Remember that making mistakes is a normal part of the learning process, and treat yourself with the same kindness and understanding that you would offer to a friend.

**Reframe negative self-talk:** Replace negative self-talk with positive affirmations. Instead of telling yourself that you're not good enough, remind yourself of your strengths and accomplishments.

**Embrace imperfection:** Recognize that perfection is unattainable and that striving for it can be harmful to your well-being. Embrace imperfection and focus on doing your best instead.

**Practice mindfulness:** Mindfulness can help you stay present in the moment and reduce anxiety and stress. Take breaks, meditate, or practice deep breathing to help you stay grounded and focused.

Remember, these strategies take time and practice to implement. Be patient with yourself and don't give up if you don't see results right away. With time and effort, you can overcome perfectionism and find a healthier, more balanced approach to life.

## Why we need healthy alternatives for perfectionism?

Once perfectionists realize that their obsession with perfectionism has exceeded healthy limits, they usually opt for one of the alternative mindsets mentioned in the preceding paragraphs. Perfectionism often leads to mental health problems, such as anxiety and depression, and can even lead to suicidal thoughts and actions. Since perfectionism creates a gap between expectations and reality, there is a risk that individuals may harm themselves or take their own lives when they cannot handle the overwhelming stress and unhappiness in their lives.

It is crucial to examine ourselves and seek assistance to make the necessary changes in our mindsets and lifestyle if perfectionism is no longer benefiting us in our daily lives and work. Remember, seeking help is not a sign of weakness, but rather a courageous step towards a happier and healthier life.

# CHAPTER 6: OVERCOMING PERFECTIONISM

After reading this book, my hope is that you feel empowered and ready to make a change in your life. However, I recognize that some of you may still choose to remain a perfectionist, and that's okay too. But if you've made it to the end of this book, chances are that perfectionism isn't working for you anymore.

Before diving into the solutions, I want to stress that there is no one-size-fits-all path to success. Each of us has our unique journey, and while some paths may be more valuable than others, there is value in every experience. The worst thing we can do is nothing. Perfectionists often struggle with this because they want to find the perfect path forward. But the truth is, there is no such thing. All we can do is choose a direction and move forward with flexibility and perseverance.

## 10 Action Steps to Take

Are you a perfectionist struggling to keep up with your personal or professional life? The good news is that you can overcome your perfectionist tendencies by following some simple steps. These are:

### Step 1: Acknowledgement

No problem can be solved without acknowledging its

existence. Remember, perfectionism is not all bad, but if it's causing issues in your life, it's time to acknowledge that it's a problem and work on fixing it.

## Step 2: Accept that you're allowed to have flaws

As humans, we all make mistakes, so don't set impossible standards for yourself or others. While you can try to improve things, don't expect perfection. Embrace your flaws and don't fear embarrassment or rejection if you make a mistake.

## Step 3: Be aware of the standards needed for the situation

Knowing the standards required for each situation can help you avoid wasting time on unnecessary tasks. So, ask for clarity and avoid making assumptions.

## Step 4: Consider worst-case scenarios

Fear of failure can often lead to inaction. Instead, think of the worst-case scenario and how unlikely it is to occur. Make a list of likely outcomes and talk it through with someone you trust to eliminate negative thoughts.

## Step 5: Take a step back from "black or white" or "all or nothing" thoughts

Life is complicated, and there are multiple ways to approach tasks. Don't let one misstep define you, and remember that everyone makes mistakes.

## Step 6: Go with the 'good enough' approach

Balance is key. Avoid getting stuck in a quest for perfection that prevents you from completing tasks. But don't use this as an excuse for mediocre work. Instead, strive for a good enough result.

## Step 7: Change your internal dialogue

Your thoughts shape your actions. As you shift away from perfectionism, pay attention to your internal dialogue and replace negative self-evaluations with positive affirmations.

## Step 8: Don't be pressurized by others' expectations

Follow your instincts, not others' standards. Take charge of your life to boost your self-esteem and reduce the power of other people's influence over you.

## Step 9: Give yourself time limits

Set deadlines to avoid endlessly working on a task.
Or work with a timer, forcing you to stop working
when it goes off.


**Step 10: Practice**

Try different strategies and find what works for you to
overcome perfectionism. Remember to keep step 6 in
mind and strive for 'good enough' instead of perfect.

# Chapter 7: The Relationship Between Perfectionism and Self-Worth

Perfectionism can have a significant impact on our self-worth and self-image. The relentless pursuit of perfection can leave us feeling like we are never good enough, leading to feelings of inadequacy and low self-esteem. In this chapter, we will explore the impact of perfectionism on self-worth and self-image, as well as strategies for building self-worth that are not tied to achievement.

## The Impact of Perfectionism on Self-Worth and Self-Image

Perfectionism is often driven by the belief that our worth as a person is tied to our achievements and accomplishments. We believe that if we can achieve perfection, then we will be worthy of love, respect, and admiration from others. However, this belief is flawed and can lead to a never-ending cycle of striving for an unattainable standard.

When we are unable to meet our perfectionistic expectations, we may begin to feel like failures or that we are not good enough. These feelings can erode our self-esteem and lead to a negative self-image. We may become overly self-critical and engage in negative self-talk, which can further damage our self-worth.

Perfectionism can also impact our relationships with others. When we are constantly striving for perfection, we may feel like we have to present a flawless image to others. This can lead to feelings of anxiety and stress, as we worry about being judged or criticized. We may also struggle to form meaningful connections with others, as we are afraid of revealing our flaws or imperfections.

## Strategies for Building Self-Worth

It is important to recognize that our self-worth is not tied to our achievements or our ability to be perfect. We are inherently valuable and deserving of love and respect, regardless of what we accomplish. Here are some strategies for building self-worth that are not tied to achievement:

**Practice self-compassion:** Self-compassion involves treating ourselves with kindness, understanding, and empathy, rather than harsh self-criticism. We can practice self-compassion by acknowledging our mistakes and shortcomings without judgment and reminding ourselves that we are doing the best we can.

**Focus on our strengths:** Instead of fixating on our flaws and weaknesses, we can focus on our strengths and positive qualities. We can make a list of our strengths and achievements and refer to it when we are feeling down or insecure.

**Engage in self-care:** Taking care of ourselves physically, mentally, and emotionally can help us feel more confident and self-assured. This can include getting enough sleep, eating a healthy diet, exercising regularly, and engaging in activities that bring us joy.

**Connect with others:** Building connections with others can help us feel a sense of belonging and worth. We can reach out to friends and family members for support and engage in activities that allow us to connect with others, such as volunteering or joining a club or group.

**Challenge negative self-talk**: When we engage in negative self-talk, we can challenge these thoughts by questioning their validity and replacing them with more positive and affirming thoughts. For example, if we find ourselves thinking, "I'm such a failure," we can challenge this thought by asking ourselves, "Is that really true? What evidence do I have to support that?"

Another important aspect of building self-worth is learning to accept ourselves, flaws and all. This can be challenging for perfectionists, who often have a difficult time accepting anything less than perfect. However, accepting our imperfections is essential for building a positive self-image and developing a healthy sense of self-worth.

One strategy for learning to accept ourselves is to practice self-acceptance. Self-acceptance involves acknowledging and embracing all aspects of ourselves, including our flaws and imperfections. It means recognizing that we are human and that we are not perfect, but that we are still worthy of love and respect.

To practice self-acceptance, we can start by identifying the areas of ourselves that we struggle to accept. We can then work to shift our mindset from one of self-criticism to one of self-acceptance. This may involve challenging negative self-talk and replacing it with more positive and affirming self-talk.

It may also involve reframing our beliefs about ourselves and our flaws. For example, instead of viewing our flaws as something to be ashamed of, we can view them as opportunities for growth and learning. By reframing our beliefs in this way, we can begin to see ourselves in a more positive light and develop a greater sense of self-worth.

In addition to practicing self-acceptance, it is also important to set realistic expectations for ourselves. Perfectionists often set impossibly high standards for themselves, which can lead to feelings of inadequacy and self-doubt. By setting realistic goals and expectations, we can reduce the pressure we put on ourselves and allow ourselves to feel more confident and self-assured.

It is also important to remember that our worth as a person is not dependent on external validation. We do not need the approval or admiration of others to be worthy of love and respect. Instead, we can learn to validate ourselves and recognize our own inherent worth and value.

Finally, it is important to seek support from others when building our self-worth. Connecting with a therapist or support group can provide a safe space to explore our feelings of self-worth and work through any underlying issues that may be contributing to our perfectionism.

Perfectionism can have a significant impact on our self-worth and self-image. However, by practicing self-compassion, focusing on our strengths, engaging in self-care, connecting with others, challenging negative self-talk, practicing self-acceptance, setting realistic expectations, validating ourselves, and seeking support, we can learn to value ourselves for who we are, not just for what we do or how well we do it. By doing so, we can cultivate a healthy sense of self-worth and develop a more positive self-image.

**Real Life Stories: Breaking the Perfectionism Cycle: How Sarah Learned to Embrace Imperfection and Achieve Self-Acceptance**

Sarah was a shining star from a very young age and continued to excel academically as she grew up. She was a high achiever and had a successful career in finance as an adult. But despite all of her accomplishments, Sarah struggled with feelings of self-doubt and insecurity.

Sarah was a perfectionist, and she had set incredibly high standards for herself. She believed that her worth as a person was directly tied to her ability to achieve and excel. She would work long hours, push herself to the limit, and make sure that everything she did was perfect.

Despite Sarah's best efforts, she was never satisfied with her work. She would relentlessly criticize herself and find flaws in everything she did. Her perfectionism had turned into a source of stress and anxiety, and it was starting to take a toll on her mental health.

One day, Sarah's boss noticed that she seemed stressed and overwhelmed. He suggested that she take some time off and seek the help of a therapist. Initially hesitant, Sarah eventually decided to give it a try.

Through therapy, Sarah learned that her worth as a person was not dependent on her achievements. She discovered that she had been using her accomplishments as a way to validate herself and prove her worth to others. She also learned that it was okay to make mistakes and that imperfection was a natural part of the human experience.

As time passed, Sarah began to change her mindset from one of self-criticism to one of self-acceptance. She learned to embrace her imperfections and recognize her own inherent worth and value. She also began to set more realistic expectations for herself and practice self-care and self-compassion.

Thanks to her therapy, Sarah was able to overcome her perfectionism and develop a more positive self-image. She continued to excel in her career, but now she did so without the pressure of trying to be perfect. Sarah learned to celebrate her successes and accept her failures as opportunities for growth and learning. Her journey serves as a reminder that our worth as individuals is not tied to our achievements, and that self-acceptance and self-compassion are crucial components of a healthy self-image.

# Chapter 8: Perfectionism in Relationships

Perfectionism can have a significant impact on personal well-being and relationships. In this chapter, we explore the effects of perfectionism on various relationships, including romantic relationships, friendships, and family dynamics. We also provide strategies for maintaining healthy relationships despite perfectionistic tendencies.

Perfectionism can create a negative dynamic in romantic relationships by leading to unrealistic expectations and disappointment. Perfectionists may struggle to accept their partner's flaws, causing them to feel criticized and undervalued. This can result in resentment and conflict. Similarly, perfectionism can also affect friendships, leading to social isolation and loneliness. Perfectionists may avoid spending time with friends who they perceive as not meeting their standards, and they may struggle with trusting their friends, fearing that they will not meet their expectations.

In families, perfectionism can create a stressful and demanding environment. Children who grow up in such an environment may struggle with low self-esteem and anxiety, feeling they must constantly meet their parents' high standards to receive love and approval. However, individuals can use various strategies to maintain healthy connections with others despite the challenges that perfectionism can pose to relationships.

One of the most important things that perfectionists can do is to practice acceptance. This means accepting themselves and others as they are, recognizing that no one is perfect, and striving for perfection is not a realistic or healthy goal. Effective communication is key to any relationship. Perfectionists may have difficulty expressing their feelings or acknowledging their mistakes, so it is important to practice open and honest communication, listening to others without judgment, and expressing oneself clearly.

Perfectionists should set realistic expectations and be flexible when things do not go as planned. Acknowledging that mistakes and setbacks are a natural part of life can help let go of the need for perfection. Practicing self-compassion can help perfectionists treat themselves with kindness and understanding. This involves acknowledging and accepting one's imperfections and mistakes, and learning to be kind to oneself in moments of difficulty.

In addition, seeking support from friends, family members, or a therapist can be helpful. A therapist can offer strategies for managing perfectionistic tendencies and improving communication skills, providing a safe and supportive space to explore and work through challenges. Practicing forgiveness towards oneself and others can also help move past mistakes and repair relationships.

Effective communication is essential for building healthy relationships. One helpful communication technique is to use "I" statements to express how the other person's actions have affected us, without putting them on the defensive. Active listening can help ensure that both parties feel heard and understood, while being open to feedback can help us improve our relationships and ourselves.

We must realize that relationships are not about being perfect, but rather showing up for each other, supporting each other, and growing together. Perfectionists may struggle with this, but practicing the above strategies can help them maintain healthy relationships despite their tendencies. By accepting imperfections, practicing effective communication, setting realistic expectations, practicing self-compassion, seeking support, and practicing forgiveness, individuals can cultivate healthy relationships with themselves and others.

## Real Life Stories: Perfectionism Puts a Strain on Jenny and John's Relationship: A Journey to Acceptance and Love

Jenny and John had been dating for six months and everything seemed to be going well. Jenny was a perfectionist who always strived for excellence in all aspects of her life, including her relationship with

John. However, her perfectionistic tendencies were beginning to put a strain on their relationship.

One evening, Jenny and John had plans to meet for dinner at a fancy restaurant. Jenny had picked out a beautiful dress and spent hours doing her hair and makeup, determined to look perfect for the occasion. When she arrived at the restaurant, she noticed that John was wearing a wrinkled shirt and had forgotten to shave. Jenny felt disappointed and embarrassed, as she felt like she had put in so much effort to look good for him.

During dinner, Jenny found herself criticizing John for his appearance, telling him that he should have put more effort into his appearance for their date. John was hurt by her comments and felt like Jenny was focusing on his flaws rather than enjoying their time together.

As the night went on, the tension between them continued to grow. Jenny felt like John didn't understand her high standards for appearance and effort, while John felt like Jenny was too critical and unaccepting of him as he was.

After that evening, Jenny and John had a long conversation about their expectations for each other and their relationship. Jenny realized that her perfectionistic tendencies were causing her to focus on John's flaws rather than appreciating him for who he was. She also realized that her high standards were unrealistic and that no one could meet them all the time.

John, on the other hand, expressed his feelings of hurt and inadequacy when Jenny criticized him for his appearance. He explained that he had been busy all day and hadn't had time to iron his shirt or shave. He also expressed his love for Jenny and his desire for her to accept him as he was, flaws and all.

After their conversation, Jenny and John were able to work through their issues and come up with strategies for maintaining a healthy relationship despite Jenny's perfectionistic tendencies. They practiced forgiveness, effective communication, and self-compassion, and their relationship grew stronger as a result. They both realized that a healthy relationship was not about being perfect, but about showing up for each other, supporting each other, and growing together.

**Some strategies for maintaining a healthy relationship that Jenny and John could have come up with are:**

**Practicing empathy**: Jenny could have tried to understand John's perspective and the reasons behind his appearance. Similarly, John could have tried to understand Jenny's perfectionistic tendencies and why they were important to her.

**Practicing acceptance:** Both Jenny and John could have worked on accepting each other as they were, flaws and all. Jenny could have recognized that John was not perfect and that it was okay, while John could have acknowledged Jenny's need for excellence and supported her in achieving her goals.

**Communicating effectively**: Jenny and John could have communicated their needs, expectations, and feelings in a non-judgmental way. They could have used "I" statements instead of "you" statements, and expressed their emotions without blaming or criticizing each other.

**Practicing self-compassion**: Jenny could have learned to be kinder to herself and accept that it was okay not to be perfect all the time. John could have supported her in this and reminded her of her worth, even when things didn't go as planned.

**Practicing forgiveness:** Jenny and John could have learned to forgive each other when mistakes were made or expectations were not met. They could have focused on the positive aspects of their relationship and worked on moving forward together.

# Chapter 9: Perfectionism in the Workplace

Perfectionism is a common trait among high-achieving individuals, and it is often seen as a positive attribute in the workplace. After all, striving for excellence can help employees produce high-quality work, meet deadlines, and achieve their goals. However, when perfectionism becomes excessive and starts to interfere with job performance and career advancement, it can have negative consequences for both employees and employers. In this chapter, we will discuss the ways in which perfectionism can affect job performance and career advancement and offer advice for finding a healthy balance between striving for excellence and avoiding burnout.

## Perfectionism and Job Performance

One of the most significant ways in which perfectionism can affect job performance is through procrastination. Perfectionists often feel overwhelmed by the high standards they set for themselves, which can lead them to delay starting or completing tasks. They may also spend an excessive amount of time on minor details, which can cause them to miss deadlines or neglect more important aspects of their work. This can lead to a decrease in productivity, job satisfaction, and overall performance.

Moreover, perfectionists may struggle with feedback and criticism. When their work is not met with approval, they may feel discouraged, defensive, or even devastated. This can make it challenging for them to accept constructive feedback, learn from their mistakes, and grow in their careers. They may also struggle to delegate tasks to others, fearing that their colleagues will not be able to meet their high standards.

Another issue that perfectionists face is the tendency to take on too much work. They may be so concerned with producing perfect results that they overcommit and take on more tasks than they can handle. This can lead to burnout, stress, and poor job performance.

## Finding a Healthy Balance

To overcome the negative effects of perfectionism on job performance, employees must learn to find a healthy balance between striving for excellence and avoiding burnout. Here are some tips for achieving this balance:

Set Realistic Goals: Instead of aiming for perfection, set realistic goals that are achievable and measurable. This will help you stay focused and motivated without feeling overwhelmed.

Prioritize Tasks: Identify the most important tasks and focus on completing them first. This will help you avoid procrastination and ensure that you are making progress on the most critical aspects of your work.

Delegate Tasks: Learn to delegate tasks to others, especially those that are not your strengths. This will help you free up time and energy to focus on your strengths and more important aspects of your work.

Embrace Feedback: Instead of fearing feedback, embrace it as an opportunity to learn and grow. Take constructive feedback as a chance to improve your skills and ask for feedback regularly.

Take Breaks: To avoid burnout, take regular breaks throughout the day. This will help you recharge your batteries, reduce stress, and increase your productivity.

Practice Self-Compassion: Instead of being hard on yourself, practice self-compassion. Be kind and forgiving to yourself when things don't go according to plan. Remember that nobody is perfect, and mistakes are an essential part of the learning process.

## Perfectionism and Career Advancement

Perfectionism can also affect career advancement. While striving for excellence can help individuals achieve their goals and advance in their careers, excessive perfectionism can lead to missed opportunities, stagnation, and even burnout. Here are some ways in which perfectionism can affect career advancement and tips for overcoming these challenges:

Fear of Failure: Perfectionists may avoid taking risks or pursuing new opportunities for fear of failure. This can lead to missed opportunities for growth and advancement. To overcome this fear, perfectionists should reframe their mindset and view failure as an opportunity to learn and grow.

Lack of Creativity: Perfectionism can also hinder creativity in the workplace. Perfectionists may become so focused on doing things the "right" way that they don't allow themselves to think outside the box and explore new ideas. This can lead to a lack of innovation and a stagnant work environment. To combat this, perfectionists should try to cultivate a more flexible and open-minded approach to problem-solving and brainstorming.

Imposter Syndrome: Perfectionists are often plagued by imposter syndrome, a feeling of inadequacy despite evidence of success. This can lead to self-doubt and a lack of confidence in the workplace, which can in turn affect job performance and career advancement. Perfectionists should acknowledge their accomplishments and remind themselves that they deserve their success.

Burnout: Perfectionists may also be at risk for burnout, as their high standards and perfectionistic tendencies can lead to overworking and a lack of work-life balance. To avoid burnout, perfectionists should prioritize self-care and set realistic goals and boundaries for themselves.

Finding a Healthy Balance: It's important for perfectionists to find a healthy balance between striving for excellence and avoiding burnout. One way to do this is to focus on progress rather than perfection. Perfectionists should acknowledge that there is always room for improvement, but that progress is more important than achieving perfection. They should also prioritize self-care and take breaks when necessary, rather than constantly pushing themselves to work harder and longer.

Another strategy for finding a healthy balance is to set realistic goals and expectations. Perfectionists should break larger goals down into smaller, more manageable tasks, and prioritize the most important ones. They should also be realistic about the amount of time and effort required to achieve their goals, and avoid setting unattainable standards for themselves.

Effective communication is also key to finding a healthy balance. Perfectionists should communicate their needs and limitations to their managers and colleagues, and be open to feedback and constructive criticism. They should also learn to delegate tasks when necessary, rather than trying to do everything themselves.

Finally, perfectionists should prioritize self-compassion and learn to accept and embrace their imperfections. They should acknowledge that making mistakes is a natural part of the learning process and view failure as an opportunity to grow and improve. By cultivating self-compassion, perfectionists can reduce their fear of failure and learn to embrace the learning process.

Perfectionism can have both positive and negative effects on job performance and career advancement. While striving for excellence and attention to detail can be beneficial, perfectionism can also lead to unrealistic expectations, fear of failure, lack of creativity, imposter syndrome, and burnout. To find a healthy balance, perfectionists should focus on progress rather than perfection, set realistic goals and expectations, communicate effectively, prioritize self-care, and cultivate self-compassion. By doing so, they can overcome the negative effects of perfectionism and achieve success in their careers while maintaining their mental and emotional well-being.

## Real Life Stories: From Perfectionism to Progress: How Sarah Found Balance and Success in the Workplace

Sarah had been a star employee at her company for three years, always showing up early, staying late, and going above and beyond her job responsibilities.

So, when her boss approached her with a new project, she was thrilled. It was a big opportunity that could take her career to the next level. However, as she worked on the project, Sarah began to feel overwhelmed. She was so focused on getting every detail perfect that she missed the deadline.

When Sarah's boss expressed his concerns about her perfectionism affecting her job performance, she was surprised. She had always thought that her perfectionism was a strength. But, her boss gave her some advice on finding a healthy balance between striving for excellence and avoiding burnout.

Taking her boss's advice, Sarah set realistic goals for herself and her projects. She learned to delegate tasks and ask for help when needed. She also started to view failure as an opportunity to learn and grow, rather than a reflection of her self-worth.

With these changes, Sarah became more productive, efficient, and happier at work. She completed her projects on time and to a high standard, and her boss was impressed with her progress.

Sarah's story demonstrates the importance of finding balance in the workplace. Perfectionism can lead to success, but it can also lead to missed opportunities, burnout, and even failure. By letting go of perfectionism and focusing on what's important, we can achieve our goals and thrive in our careers. So, let's strive for excellence, but let's also remember to take care of ourselves and enjoy the journey.

# CHAPTER 10: PERFECTIONISM AND CREATIVITY

Perfectionism and creativity are often considered desirable traits for high achievers. However, they can also be a source of conflict. In creative fields, perfectionism can be paralyzing, leading individuals to second-guess themselves and their ideas. On the other hand, creativity requires a willingness to take risks, experiment with new ideas, and tolerate uncertainty and ambiguity. Extreme perfectionism can undermine creativity by causing individuals to focus more on avoiding mistakes and meeting impossible standards than on exploring new ideas and taking risks.

A study by Lisa M. Baird and colleagues found that a balance between setting high standards and allowing for experimentation and risk-taking is key to harnessing creative energy while managing perfectionistic tendencies. The study also revealed that adaptive perfectionism, characterized by high standards and striving for excellence, was positively associated with creativity. In contrast, maladaptive perfectionism, characterized by fear of failure and excessive self-criticism, was negatively associated with creativity.

To achieve a balance between perfectionism and creativity, individuals can set realistic goals and expectations, recognizing that perfection is unattainable and that mistakes and failures are a natural part of the creative process. Focusing on the process rather than the outcome is another strategy. Creativity is a journey, and the focus should be on enjoying the experience and learning from it. Practicing self-compassion is also important, treating oneself with kindness and understanding rather than harsh self-criticism. Seeking support and feedback from others, such as mentors or colleagues, can also provide guidance and encouragement.

It is important to note that perfectionism and creativity are not mutually exclusive, and in fact, they can complement each other when managed effectively. A healthy dose of perfectionism can push individuals to strive for excellence and achieve their creative goals, while creativity can help individuals to break free from rigid standards and find innovative solutions. The key is to strike a balance between the two and manage perfectionism so that it does not hinder the creative process.

In conclusion, perfectionism and creativity can be complex, and it is important to understand how they interact in order to manage their impact on creative pursuits. While perfectionism and creativity can conflict, it is possible to harness creative energy without getting bogged down by perfectionistic tendencies. By setting realistic goals and expectations, focusing on the process, practicing self-compassion, and seeking support, individuals can achieve balance and unleash their creative potential. It is important to remember that creativity is not about being perfect but rather about exploring and experimenting with new ideas, and that mistakes and failures are an integral part of the process. With this understanding, individuals can cultivate a creative mindset and achieve their goals without sacrificing their mental well-being.

## Strategies for managing the conflict between perfectionism and creativity

**Set realistic goals and expectations**: Recognize that perfection is unattainable and that mistakes and failures are a natural part of the creative process. Set realistic goals and expectations that allow for experimentation and risk-taking.

**Focus on the process rather than the outcome:** Rather than focusing solely on the end result, focus on the journey and enjoy the experience of exploring new ideas and concepts.

**Practice self-compassion**: Treat oneself with kindness and understanding, rather than harsh self-criticism. Remember that making mistakes is a natural part of the creative process and that failure is an opportunity to learn and grow.

**Seek support and feedback:** Seek guidance and encouragement from others, such as mentors or colleagues. Collaborating with others can provide new perspectives and ideas, as well as support when facing challenges.

**Embrace imperfection:** Accept that imperfection is a natural part of the creative process and can be a source of inspiration. Allow oneself to make mistakes and learn from them.

**Practice adaptive perfectionism:** Strive for excellence and high standards while allowing for experimentation and risk-taking. Recognize that perfectionism can be beneficial in certain fields, but maladaptive perfectionism can be detrimental to creativity.

By employing these strategies, individuals can strike a balance between perfectionism and creativity, harness creative energy, and achieve their creative goals. It is important to remember that creativity is a journey, not a destination, and that it requires taking risks, tolerating uncertainty, and embracing imperfection.


# Real Life Stories: The Paralysis of Perfectionism: How My Fear of Failure Hindered My Creativity


One anecdote that illustrates the conflict between perfectionism and creativity is that of Pablo Picasso, one of the most influential artists of the 20th century. Picasso was known for his innovative and unconventional approach to art, which often involved distorting and abstracting the human form. However, he also had a perfectionistic streak, and would sometimes spend weeks or even months on a single painting, striving to achieve his desired level of perfection.

One such painting was Les Demoiselles d'Avignon, which he worked on for nearly a year. Picasso was so obsessed with getting every detail right that he made countless sketches and studies, and even destroyed earlier versions of the painting when he wasn't satisfied with them. His perfectionism caused him to doubt his own abilities and the direction of the work, leading to a period of creative stagnation and self-doubt.

Eventually, Picasso realized that his quest for perfection was hindering his creativity and preventing him from exploring new ideas. He began to embrace the imperfections and mistakes in his work, using them as opportunities for experimentation and discovery. This led to a period of great creative output and innovation, and his work continued to push the boundaries of traditional art.

Picasso's story illustrates how perfectionism can be a double-edged sword for creative individuals. While striving for excellence can drive one to create great work, it can also lead to self-doubt and creative stagnation. It is only by embracing imperfection, taking risks, and allowing for experimentation that true creative potential can be unleashed.

# CHAPTER 11: THE INTERSECTION OF PERFECTIONISM AND CULTURE

Perfectionism is a personality trait influenced by various factors, including cultural norms and values. Culture can shape the way individuals view and approach perfectionism. Cultural factors such as individualism, collectivism, and high power distance play significant roles in shaping perfectionistic tendencies. This chapter examines how cultural norms and values contribute to perfectionistic tendencies and highlights the experiences of individuals from different cultural backgrounds.

Individualism, which emphasizes individual autonomy and self-expression, contributes to perfectionistic tendencies by promoting the idea that individuals are solely responsible for their success. In contrast, collectivism emphasizes the importance of group harmony and interdependence, and mistakes and failures are viewed as a reflection of the group rather than the individual. High power distance, which refers to the degree to which power and status are distributed unequally in a society, promotes the idea that individuals must meet the high expectations of those in authority.

The relationship between culture and perfectionism is complex, and individuals from different cultural backgrounds may experience and express perfectionistic tendencies differently. While cultural factors can contribute to perfectionistic tendencies, they do not determine an individual's level of perfectionism. Cultural values can change over time and across generations.

Individualistic cultures may contribute to perfectionistic tendencies by promoting the ideal of individual achievement and competition. Success is often measured by personal accomplishments, such as high grades, prestigious careers, and material possessions. This can create pressure to excel and outperform others, which can fuel perfectionistic tendencies. Furthermore, the emphasis on self-reliance and independence can lead to a reluctance to seek help or support, which can exacerbate feelings of self-doubt and isolation.

On the other hand, collectivistic cultures may also contribute to perfectionistic tendencies by placing a strong emphasis on social harmony and conformity. Success is often measured by one's ability to conform to social expectations and maintain positive relationships with others. This can create pressure to fit in and avoid mistakes or failures that could jeopardize social relationships. Seeking help or support may be stigmatized as a sign of weakness or a burden on others, which can prevent individuals from seeking the resources they need to manage perfectionistic tendencies.

Research shows that individuals from different cultural backgrounds experience perfectionistic tendencies differently. For example, Asian Americans are more likely to report perfectionistic tendencies than

European Americans, due to cultural values that emphasize diligence, hard work, and academic achievement. African Americans may experience perfectionistic tendencies related to social expectations and cultural stereotypes, while Latinx individuals may experience lower levels of perfectionism due to cultural values that prioritize relationships and social connections over individual achievement.

In conclusion, perfectionism is a complex personality trait influenced by cultural norms and values. Cultural factors such as individualism, collectivism, and high power distance can contribute to perfectionistic tendencies, and individuals from different cultural backgrounds experience perfectionistic tendencies differently. It is essential to recognize the intersection of culture and perfectionism to provide better support and resources for individuals struggling with perfectionistic tendencies.

## Real Life Stories: The Tale of Two Cousins: How Culture Shapes Perfectionism

There were two cousins who grew up in different parts of the world. One, named John, grew up in the United States, where individualism is highly valued. The other, named Li, grew up in China, where collectivism is more emphasized.

As children, both John and Li were high achievers in school and always strived for perfection in everything they did. However, as they grew older, they began to approach their perfectionism in different ways due to their cultural backgrounds.

John, living in an individualistic culture, felt a constant pressure to succeed and outperform others. He put a lot of pressure on himself to be the best in his class and excel in extracurricular activities. He was hesitant to ask for help or support from others, as he felt it was a sign of weakness or that he wasn't living up to societal expectations.

On the other hand, Li, growing up in a collectivistic culture, felt pressure to conform to social expectations and maintain positive relationships with others. She was hesitant to take risks or make mistakes, as she felt it could jeopardize her relationships with others. Seeking help or support was also stigmatized in her culture, as it was seen as burdening others and potentially disrupting social harmony.

Years later, John and Li met up during a family gathering. They discussed their experiences with perfectionism and how their cultural backgrounds shaped their approach to it. John realized that seeking help and support from others is not a sign of weakness, but rather a strength that can help him achieve his goals. Li learned that making mistakes and taking risks can lead to personal growth and self-improvement.

The two cousins recognized that while cultural factors can contribute to perfectionistic tendencies, they do not determine an individual's level of perfectionism. They acknowledged that everyone can struggle with perfectionism, regardless of their cultural background, and that it is essential to recognize the intersection of culture and perfectionism to provide better support and resources for those who struggle with it.

## Navigating Cultural Perceptions of Perfectionism: Considerations for Working with Diverse Populations

When working with individuals from different cultures who struggle with perfectionism, it is important to be aware of how cultural norms and values may influence their attitudes and behaviors. Here are some issues that people working with different cultures must be aware of when it comes to perfectionism:

Understanding different cultural perspectives on perfectionism: It is important to recognize that the way perfectionism is viewed and experienced may vary across cultures. For example, in individualistic cultures, perfectionism may be viewed as a desirable trait, while in collectivistic cultures, it may be seen as a negative attribute.

Being aware of different cultural approaches to seeking help: In some cultures, seeking help or support may be seen as a sign of weakness, while in others, it may be viewed as a way of demonstrating humility and respect for others. People working with different cultures should be aware of these attitudes and be prepared to provide different types of support depending on the cultural context.

Recognizing the impact of cultural expectations on perfectionism: Cultural expectations may contribute to perfectionistic tendencies, such as the pressure to conform to social norms or the emphasis on individual achievement. People working with different cultures should be aware of these expectations and the impact they may have on an individual's perfectionism.

Being sensitive to the impact of cultural stereotypes: Cultural stereotypes may influence an individual's experience of perfectionism, particularly in cases where stereotypes suggest that members of certain cultural groups should be high achievers or have certain traits. People working with different cultures should be aware of these stereotypes and be careful not to reinforce them.

Being respectful of cultural values: Cultural values such as respect, harmony, and humility may influence an individual's approach to perfectionism. People working with different cultures should be respectful of these values and be prepared to adapt their approach accordingly.

Overall, working with individuals from different cultures who struggle with perfectionism requires sensitivity to cultural differences and a willingness to adapt one's approach to meet the needs of the individual. By recognizing the impact of cultural norms and values on perfectionism, people can better support individuals who struggle with this issue.

# CHAPTER 12: OVERCOMING PERFECTIONISM: TIPS & ROADBLOCKS

Overcoming perfectionism is an ongoing process that requires dedication, commitment, and a willingness to make changes in one's thinking and behavior. This chapter provides tips for staying motivated and committed to the process of overcoming perfectionism, as well as common roadblocks to progress and how to overcome them.

## Tips for Staying Motivated and Committed to Overcoming Perfectionism:

- Set realistic goals and break down larger goals into smaller, achievable steps.
- Track progress by writing down accomplishments, challenges, and areas for improvement.
- Seek support from friends, family, or a therapist to provide accountability and motivation.
- Practice self-care through exercise, healthy eating, relaxation techniques, and engaging in fulfilling activities.
- Practice mindfulness techniques, such as meditation or yoga, to increase awareness of

thoughts and emotions and reduce stress and anxiety.

## Common Roadblocks to Progress and How to Overcome Them:

- All-or-nothing thinking: Challenge extreme thoughts and ask yourself if they are accurate or supported by evidence.
- Fear of failure: Reframe failure as an opportunity for growth and learning.
- Self-criticism: Practice self-compassion and treat yourself with kindness and understanding.
- Procrastination: Break tasks into smaller steps, set deadlines, and hold yourself accountable by sharing progress with others or seeking support from a therapist or coach.
- Perfectionistic standards: Practice setting realistic and achievable standards and accept that mistakes and imperfections are a natural part of the learning process.
- Relapse is another common roadblock to progress in overcoming perfectionism. It is important to recognize that setbacks are a natural part of the process of change and develop a plan for dealing with them in advance. This plan should include strategies for managing negative emotions, seeking support, and getting back on track.

It is also important to celebrate successes along the way and recognize that overcoming perfectionism is not a one-time event but rather an ongoing process. Even after significant progress has been made, it is important to continue practicing self-care, seeking support, and challenging perfectionistic thinking.

In conclusion, maintaining progress in overcoming perfectionism requires a commitment to the process of change, a willingness to adapt and make changes, and a focus on long-term goals. By setting realistic goals, tracking progress, seeking support, practicing self-care and mindfulness, and challenging perfectionistic thinking, progress can be maintained. Common roadblocks to progress, such as all-or-nothing thinking, fear of failure, self-criticism, procrastination, and perfectionistic standards, can be overcome by developing a plan for dealing with setbacks, celebrating successes, and recognizing that overcoming perfectionism is an ongoing process.


## Real Life Stories: Overcoming Perfectionism: Emily's Journey to a Fulfilling Life

Emily was an ambitious young woman named Emily who had a strong desire to excel at everything she did, but this often caused her a great deal of stress and anxiety. However, one day, Emily decided to take control of her perfectionism and lead a more fulfilling life.

She discovered valuable tips to help her overcome her perfectionism, and she set realistic goals for herself. Emily learned to break down larger goals into smaller, achievable steps, and she celebrated her successes along the way.

Of course, there were some obstacles along the way. But Emily worked with a therapist who helped her reframe failure as an opportunity for growth and learning. She also practiced self-compassion, treating herself with kindness and understanding.

As time passed, Emily made significant progress in overcoming her perfectionism. She realized that mistakes and imperfections are a natural part of the learning process, and she no longer felt like she had to do everything perfectly. Emily continued to practice self-care and mindfulness and developed a plan to deal with setbacks whenever they arose.

In the end, Emily was proud of herself for the progress she had made. She realized that overcoming perfectionism is a lifelong journey, but the effort was undoubtedly worth it. Now, she lives a more balanced, fulfilling life, and she encourages others to take the first step towards overcoming their own perfectionism.

# EPILOGUE

Congratulations! You've come a long way in your journey towards overcoming perfectionism. Taking the first step towards recognizing that perfectionism can be a barrier to success and happiness is a significant accomplishment in itself. It's time to reflect on your journey so far, celebrate your successes, and chart your next steps towards a more fulfilling life.

As you look back on your journey, you might notice how far you've come. Maybe you've started giving yourself permission to make mistakes or be less than perfect, or you've let go of some unrealistic expectations. Perhaps you've learned to prioritize self-care and take breaks when you need them. Whatever progress you've made, take a moment to acknowledge and celebrate it. Celebrating your successes can help boost your confidence and motivate you to keep going.

Now, it's time to plan your next steps. Think about the areas in which you'd like to continue to work on, and set some achievable goals. Maybe you want to learn to ask for help when you need it, or you want to start a new hobby that doesn't have to be perfect. Perhaps you want to work on being more mindful and present in the moment. Whatever your goals are, make sure they're realistic and measurable. Break them down into smaller steps that you can tackle one at a time.

Remember that overcoming perfectionism is a journey, and it's not something that happens overnight. Be patient with yourself and celebrate your progress along the way. Embrace the mistakes you make as opportunities to learn and grow. Keep in mind that setbacks will happen, but that's okay. Keep pushing forward, and remember that progress, not perfection, is the goal.

As you continue on your journey towards overcoming perfectionism, surround yourself with supportive and encouraging people. Seek out role models who inspire you and who have been successful in overcoming perfectionism themselves. Join support groups or find a therapist who can help you navigate your journey.

Finally, remember to enjoy the journey! Overcoming perfectionism can be challenging, but it can also be incredibly rewarding. Embrace the process, celebrate your successes, and keep moving forward. With each step, you're getting closer to living a more fulfilling, balanced, and joyful life. Congratulations on your progress so far, and best of luck on your continued journey!

Thank you for purchasing and reading this book. I really hope you got a lot out of it. Please take a few moments to leave a review for this book on Amazon by scanning the QR code below. I am always looking for ways to improve my publications and your feedback is invaluable.

Please leave a review. Thank you!